Friendly Tales

Ian Buckett

This edition first published in paperback by
Michael Terence Publishing in 2024
www.mtp.agency

ISBN 9781800948747

Michael Terence
Publishing

Contents

Friendly Tales

In a tree a squirrel lived
And Sammy was his name
The tree was large and it did give
To Sammy that much shelter

At the foot of that large tree
Someone had made a hole
His name was Browncoat and he was
A very furry vole

And there within that little wood
A hedgehog he did live
His name was Prickles and his home
Was where the holly stood

Children, the poem above is just an introduction to the characters in the following stories and before I launch on them perhaps a little more explanation is needed.

The stories are primarily for you although grown-ups are more than welcome to join in the fun and enjoy them and perhaps find some release from the ever-increasing toils of their own world in another world all of which is rural and regrettably now mostly in the past.

The characters about which I shall write are Sammy, Browncoat, and Prickles.

Sammy is a grey squirrel who lives in a drey at the top of an old oak tree and feeds mainly on nuts and seeds and occasional berries all the year round. Although he is a lot more sleepy in the winter when the warm sun leaves and the clouds make it chilly. He is the leader of the trio as he is very smart and has good ideas.

Browncoat is a vole with a brown and very furry coat who lives in a hole at the foot of the oak tree in which Sammy lives. He feeds mainly on hazelnuts and blackberries along with other fruit and insects and remains active in the winter months running very quickly from place to place and therefore acts as a warning guard for the wood.

Prickles is a hedgehog who lives under some holly bushes, where he buries himself in the winter to sleep. He feeds on worms, slugs, and snails that he easily finds in the soft dirt around him. He also moves a lot faster than you might think by looking at him.

The wood is on top of a grassy hill which gently slopes up like a big mound. The wood is deciduous (which means the trees lose their leaves in Autumn, and they grow back in Spring) and has mainly oak and beech trees, with a few chestnut trees and, lower down, hazel and holly bushes.

If you look really hard, you'll also find brambles (that have delicious blackberries and raspberries from summer into Autumn) and plenty of wild flowers.

One side of the grassy hill has a gravel path that you could walk on but isn't used by cars. But the hill is far from any homes, except for a few farms, so very few people bother it. On two sides, there are fences separating it from fields where animals graze or crops grow, and on the other side, there's a small river.

Next to the wood, lower down the hill on the north side, there is a copse (a small group of trees) called the wildwood. It is mainly coniferous (trees which keep their leaves all year round), with a few straggly oaks. Wildwood is dark and home to predators such as foxes, stoats, and weasels, and in the trees, ravens and crows make their nests.

Between the two facing south there is a well populated rabbit warren and a little further away a badger's sett.

1

Down by the Riverside

The spring was upon the wood and the sun was shining sufficiently for the weather to cast off the last vestiges of winter and bring some warmth. It chanced that one morning brighter than the ones of recent days Sammy awoke, stretched, and yawned. He thought to himself 'I wonder what Browncoat and Prickles are doing particularly if Prickles has woken up?' So he left the dray and climbed down the oak tree with his tail in the air as squirrels do and when he reached the ground looked to see if there was anyone to be seen. As he was unable to find anyone after a time he called out 'come on you lazy lot, it's a fine day and we should be doing things.'

At that Browncoat appeared saying with a grin 'Lazy yourself, I've been awake all winter and been very busy making sure that we have no unwelcome visitors so let's go and see if Prickles is around yet.'

So off the two friends went to the holly bushes where Prickles lived and gave him a shout. After a while a grumpy voice said 'Why are you disturbing my sleep? It isn't time to get up yet so please go away.' Sammy laughed and replied that it certainly is time and that Prickles was the last creature of the year to wake and if he didn't hurry he would miss the spring completely. 'Humph' said Prickles as he grudgingly arose and came out from under the holly bushes 'so what are we going to do then?'

Sammy thought for a moment and then said 'Why don't we go down to the river and see how it has survived the winter?' 'That's a good idea' said Browncoat as none of them had been there since the previous autumn when they had enjoyed sitting in the last of the summer sun and watching all the birdlife. So off they set down from the wood and headed across the grassy slope towards the foot of the hill where the river meandered its course from the higher hills on its way though the town to the sea. When they reached the foot of the hill they spread out to explore what was happening. Sammy called out 'be careful not to fall in or get stuck in the mud.'

Browncoat being quick explored amongst the rushes and was pleased to see that they had survived the winter and were growing well and Sammy nosed around the bank to see if the winter had affected it and just where the water level was.

Suddenly there was a shout from the bank just up from Sammy and Browncoat. Both of them looked up as the shout sounded like Prickles who since having woken had cast off his bad mood and was even keener than the other two to find out what was going on. 'Hey look what I've found' shouted Prickles so the other two ran over to see what was going on and found Prickles on the edge of the riverbank just beside a bridge which up until then had escaped the notice of both Sammy and Browncoat. The bridge was built in such a way that when the current slackened debris collected by the support nearest the bank and as there had not been much rain the river level was low and amongst other debris a small timber board had become wedged between the support and the bank and it was this that had made Prickles shout.

'Now we can have some fun' said Prickles 'we can sit on that board and enjoy actually being on the river in absolute safety.' 'I'm not so sure about that said Sammy doubtfully as that board is not in any way moored and could float off at any time.' 'Nonsense' replied Prickles 'it looks quite safe to me as the board is wedged against the bridge and after all we have come out to find adventure so I think you are being over-cautious and to prove it I'll show you what I mean.' Then before either Sammy or Browncoat could say any more Prickles jumped from the river bank on to the board.

'There you are he shouted, safe as houses' but what he had failed to notice that as the board was not in any way moored it would not take much movement to dislodge it and so it was that before he knew it the board with its additional load had shifted its position and began to float out on to the river current. Noticing this Prickles began to panic. 'Do something' he shouted to Sammy and Browncoat as the board started to move towards the centre of the river but there was nothing that they could do and looked at one another with some concern.

Sammy was the first to recover and said to Browncoat 'There's another bridge over the river further round the foot of the hill which is similar to this one and there are swans living there who may be able to help.' 'That's fine said Browncoat but can we get there before Prickles is swept past?' 'Yes said

Sammy as the river is flowing slowly and you and I can run quite fast so let's get going before it's too late.

In the meanwhile, Prickles was now in the centre of the river and moving slowly downstream. 'Oh dear' he said 'before I know it I shall reach the sea and before it does I believe the river flows through a town and goodness knows what there is there. Oh how I wish I hadn't got on this board but too late for that now.'

By now Sammy and Browncoat had run well ahead of Prickles and were in sight of the bridge that Sammy knew about and sure enough just before it there were two swans swimming gently.

'Hey there can you help us please?' called out Sammy. 'Our friend Prickles the hedgehog is afloat on a board and in danger of being swept out to sea unless something is done and neither of us can swim well enough to help.'

The swans looked up in surprise. 'A hedgehog on a board whatever next' they said 'we've seen some peculiar things in our time here but never anything like that but what can we do to help?' Sammy called back 'when he appears your wings are large enough to shepherd the board back to the safety of the bank so could you do that please?' The swans said 'well that's easy and rather than use the bank we will lodge him against the bridge support where there will be no risk of him being swept away. 'Excellent idea' said Sammy so they all settled down and waited for Prickles to come into sight.

In the meanwhile, Prickles had got over his initial panic and was trying to think as to how he could get himself back to the bank but he failed to see two glinting eyes from the bank opposite the hill. Those eyes belonged to an otter which had spotted Prickle's dilemma and whilst recognising that a hedgehog would not make a good meal decided that it would have some rather malicious fun. So the otter jumped into the river and swam up to Prickles on his board who was being carried slowly onwards.

'Hello Mr Hedgehog so what are you doing in the river? It's not really your place or maybe you have learned to swim and need a hand to get off of that board perhaps?' The otter then chuckled and moved towards Prickles who looked suspiciously at him and was becoming alarmed as to his intentions.

The otter meanwhile was nosing at the board and saying 'Now let's see if hedgehogs can swim.'

Prickles became even more alarmed and said in his sternest voice 'go away as I certainly do not wish to swim today' but the otter took no notice and merely said 'come on in, the water is beautiful and I have never seen a hedgehog swim before' and then kept on nosing at the board harder and harder trying to tip Prickles into the river. Prickles by now had resigned himself to being tipped in the water by the mischievous otter and was by no means confident of being able to swim as far as the bank as he had developed a great deal of fat during the winter months but just as he was about to give up he heard a shout from down-river.

During the scuffle between Prickles and the otter neither of them had noticed that the flow of the river had carried them round the curve of the hill and that they were now in sight of the bridge where the swans were waiting and where Sammy and Browncoat were also looking on from the bank. For a moment the swans had not seen the otter which was no friend of theirs as over the years it had both played tricks and chased their signets and the shout was purely because they had spotted Prickles and were making ready to guide him to safety.

On hearing the shout the otter stopped trying to spill Prickles into the river and seeing the swans bearing down on him immediately tried to make his escape but he was too late as the swans had reached the board and with their wingspan cut off the otter from safety. 'Now we've got you' they said and this time you are going to pay for your mischief which has been going on for far too long.

Otters however are known to be swift and this one was both swift and alert so he dived under the swans and before they could do anything about it he was off into the river but unfortunately at this point the river narrowed slightly and so the current quickened and carried him downstream at such a rate that he was unable to find his way to either bank and was swept on downriver towards the sea. Before he knew it the river had left the countryside and carried him through the local town but fortunately for him no-one saw him and he was carried along on the current towards the mouth of the river and the sea. 'Oh what is to become of me' moaned the otter 'it would have been much better if I had stayed in my holt and not been tempted into the river but too late now so I will just have to see where the river takes me.'

At that point the river joined with the sea and at its mouth lived a family of sea otters some of whom chanced to be fishing when the otter appeared. 'Goodness' said one of them 'what a sight you are wherever have you been and where have you come from?' The otter whose name was Slinky then introduced himself with some relief at finding kindred spirits and recounted his adventures albeit with some omissions as he had no wish to be turned away and face the tiring trip back up-river which he was not at all sure that he could manage. The sea otters gathered round and said to him 'it is clear from what you say that you have lessons to learn so what are your circumstances and do you have a family?' Slinky replied that he lived alone in a holt further up-river and there was no particular reason for him to return so he asked the sea otters 'could I possibly stay here and join you as I have always wanted a family and perhaps that would stop me making mischief.' The sea otters thought about it for a while and the chief otter then said to Slinky 'it is very clear that you have lived a strange life up to now and are sadly in need of some training to put a stop to your mischief making and as it happens we are currently low on numbers so yes you can join us and perhaps we can teach you a better way of conducting yourself as we do not interfere with other animals although we do hunt fish to eat and can show you how it is done.' Slinky thought about this and made a decision. 'Yes I would like to stay and am very grateful for your offer and will make every effort to mend my ways.' So here children we will leave Slinky and the sea otters and return to the friends who were still by the bridge over the river.

In the meanwhile, the swans called out to Sammy and Browncoat 'there is no danger now that the otter has gone so we will help your friend back to the bank.' With that they ushered both the board and Prickles towards the safety of the bridge support where they both came to a halt. 'Thank you very much' said Prickles to the swans 'w … don't know what I should have done … said the swans 'in a peculiar way you … favour as we have been trying to rid the river of … wretched otter as it has been making mischief for far too long and now almost certainly will not be able to return so we have done each other a favour.' At that they gently manoeuvred the board to the bank whilst still protected by the support where Sammy and Browncoat were waiting and who also added their thanks as they had watched the events with considerable misgivings as they had been quite unable to help and between them they brought Prickles off the board and onto the safety of the bank. 'Goodbye' they called to the swans 'and again our thanks.' 'Think nothing of it after all it has been quite an adventure and we don't have many of them these days so we must now be off back to our cygnets as they will wonder where we have been.'

Prickles shook himself and said to Sammy and Browncoat 'thank goodness for swans and dry land otherwise I should have been finished by that otter.' 'Yes you would you stupid hedgehog and in doing what you did without rhyme or reason you have put all of us through a great deal of work and worry which could easily have been avoided if you had but listened to us.' Prickles hearing this was very wncast. 'I am dreadfully sorry but after such a ,ong winter I was full of energy and just wanted to have some fun but can see now that it was rather silly as I am not at all a good swimmer and would have been in trouble had I been tipped off of that board and in even more if the swans had not rescued me so again my apologies.' Sammy and Browncoat were pleased with Prickle's apology but Sammy was still annoyed so he said to Prickles 'very well apology accepted so behave yourself in future and follow us back to the wood where there is no more water for you to play in.'

So off the three of them went back up the hill with Sammy in front and Prickles looking rather downcast tagging behind Browncoat. By then the day was well on and the sun whilst still warm was past its midday peak so all three were keen to get back to the shade of the wood and as none of them had eaten since breakfast find nuts, berries, and grubs to rid themselves of the pangs of hunger. Up the hill they went until they reached the outskirts of the wood along which there grew a fairly thick band of bushes along with brambles which formed a protective barrier. By this time Prickles being the slowest of the three and also the least hungry due to his winter fat had fallen a little way behind the other two who were both just reaching the fringes of the wood.

As they approached the bushes there was a sudden commotion and to their great surprise sprang two rangy looking cats both with mean green eyes and clearly meaning trouble.

Neither Sammy nor Browncoat hesitated as both knew trouble when they saw it. Sammy dived through the bushes and straight up the nearest tree and Browncoat also scuttled through the bushes and finding a disused hole dived in. 'Bother' said one of the cats 'there goes tea as neither of us can dig and although we can climb the squirrel is better at it than us.' At that moment Prickles appeared and was spotted by the second cat who with an evil smile said to his friend 'wait a moment all is not lost and we might yet have some tea.' So they both advanced on Prickles with that stealthy look common to all cats when hunting. Prickles for his part understood immediately what was happening and said to the cats 'be careful what you wish for as hedgehogs are not so easily overcome.' 'That's nonsense' said both cats 'we are larger and stronger than you and we intend staying in this wood to hunt whatever lives here.' 'Oh do you just' said Prickles backing away a little 'well I'll give you a taste of what happens to those who are not welcome here.' So without further ado Prickles ran at the first cat as fast as he could and when he was within striking distance rolled himself into a ball and hurled himself at the cat who did not have the time to get out of the way and so found himself struck fair and square.

Prickles was then buried in the cat's fur but more importantly his prickly coat was embedded in the cat's skin underneath its fur. The cat let out a howl of distress and shook himself as hard as he could to rid himself of Prickles which after a struggle he managed to do.

'I'll get you for that' snarled the second cat and he launched himself at Prickles but Prickles curled up in a ball again just as the cat struck with the same result as had happened previously so there was yet another howl and the cat shaking himself free swiftly backed off. Prickles now had the upper hand and advanced towards the cats who looked angrily at him whilst waving their tails. 'Would you like some more' said Prickles menacingly because if you would there is me and all my relatives and we live here all the time so beware.

The cats looked at one another and then at Prickles who thought to himself that he hoped they would believe him as if they both attacked at once he was done for but luckily the cats thought better of it and with another snarl headed back down the hill whilst licking their wounds. 'Well that didn't work very well did it?' said one cat to the other 'so perhaps we had better leave the wood alone if that is the reception that we shall get.' 'I think so as well' said the second cat so they both headed back to the farm from which they had come and were not seen again in the wood.

Meanwhile, Prickles rather shakily picked himself up and at the same time Sammy and Browncoat re-appeared. 'Are you alright?' asked Sammy to which Prickles replied 'Yes thanks I am now.' 'That was very well done' said Sammy 'that coat of yours does have its uses which I would never have suspected and if it hadn't we would all have been done for so I think you should go to the top of the class and forget all about rivers as you are well and truly forgiven' 'Hear hear' said Browncoat' we are both soft skinned and have no chance against cat's claws and teeth so that coat of yours is a godsend but just the same I will keep a sharp eye out in case they return although I suspect that they have had enough especially if they believe that line about your relatives which was clever of you.'

And with that as by now the sun was waning the three friends went back into the wood to find their tea after which they all took a well-earned rest.

All three friends they woke with the spring
And all gathered round in a ring
Then off they went out
To see what was about
Those adventurous friends in the spring

Sammy
Browncoat
Prickles

2

A Tale of Many Rabbits

It was early summer and the mornings were waking with a smile. The trees had clothed their winter skeletons with a sheen of leaves which was developing from the earlier slivers of light green and was rapidly providing both shade and cover for all those who lived in the wood.

One such bright morning Sammy awoke and said to himself' I cannot remain in my drey any longer, I must go and see what Browncoat and Prickles are doing.' So he scuttled down the tree and looked for Browncoat but he was not to be seen. 'He must be doing his rounds' thought Sammy and just at that moment Browncoat appeared along with Prickles. 'Where have you been' said Browncoat 'it's a lovely day and both of us were up early and have had a good look around the wood to see that all is well.'

'That's good' said Sammy 'and did you find anything?' 'Nothing out of the ordinary' said Browncoat 'except that there are a lot of rabbits out on the hill above their warren.' 'Oh' said Sammy 'that's interesting so let's go and see what they are up to' and with that he led the way to the edge of the wood where they could see a great deal of rabbits feeding on the clover in the sun. As the three friends appeared in sight one of the nearest rabbits seeing them stopped eating and stamped on the ground. At that all the other rabbits also stopped eating and scampered back towards their warren with the exception of the rabbit who had spotted them who stopped and shouted to the other rabbits 'it's alright they are not from the wild wood and are friends of ours.'

He then said to the three friends 'I'm sorry about that but we have heard rumours that those who live in the wild wood are stirring and they are no friends of ours.' 'My name is Thumper' said the rabbit 'and I act as lookout for the warren and although I have seen the vole before as he was clearly on his rounds I don't know the other two of you.'

Sammy then introduced the three of them to Thumper and asked as to how many rabbits there were in the warren and how long had they been there and was there a leader. 'Goodness' said Thumper 'what a lot of questions but now that you are clearly not a threat to us I think that the best way of answering you is to invite you to the warren so that you can see how we live so could you come at midday and I will meet you by the wood to guide you?' 'That's very kind of you' said Sammy so he turned to Browncoat and Prickles and said 'shall we go?' at which the two of them said 'oh yes what fun it's been a while since we have been out on the hill so it will make a nice change' 'That's settled then' said Thumper and off he went back to the warren and the three friends went back into the wood to prepare for their outing.

In the meantime, over in the wild wood things were indeed stirring as Thumper had feared. The wild wood itself was a windswept and lonely place where a number of ragged pines grew closely together interspersed with a few deciduous trees reaching desperately upwards to the light. The pines were home to a number of crows and ravens which made their nests at the top of them where they could see out onto the rest of the hill and keep an eye on the movements of others. The floor of the wood was covered with many years' accumulation of pine needles and was generally dry as the rain had difficulty in penetrating through the trees and it was also dark as the light had a similar problem and unlike the wood at the top of the hill was not carpeted with any flowers.

In the wood lived foxes, stoats, and weasels all of whom preyed on others for food and were therefore particularly unpleasant to their neighbours. On this day they had decided to meet to see how they could expand their territory beyond the wild wood 'It's about time that we ruled all of the hill and then could hunt wherever we like' said the foxes 'the rabbits would provide many good meals for all of us and if we were clever we could leave enough of them to keep on providing us with food forever. 'Excellent thinking' said the stoats and the weasels agreed 'but what about those who live in the wood at the top of the hill and also the badgers?' 'We are quite strong enough to deal with the wood at the top of the hill and the badgers will not want to interfere' said the foxes 'so why wait as no-one will be expecting us to attack' The others thought for a while but clearly found the proposal appealing so it was agreed that they would wait until midday when the rabbits returned to their warren and ask the crows and ravens to let them know when the hill was clear so that they could cross the open space between the wild wood and the warren without being seen. One of the foxes then called to the nearest raven and explained what they had in mind adding that they would share with them the plunder so the birds readily agreed and positioned themselves as lookouts while the fox reported back to the rest of the conspirators. 'All very good' they said so now all we have to do is wait and then advance when no-one is looking.

In the meanwhile, back in the wood at the top of the hill the three friends were making ready for their visit to the rabbit warren. Unable to contain their excitement they had all talked to their relatives of whom the squirrels and particularly the hedgehogs were keen to join them but Sammy after thinking said that the sensible way forward would be for the three of them to go so as not to frighten the rabbits with too many of them and they could ask if others could visit on a later date. They all agreed to this providing that those of their relatives who wished could wait at the edge of the wood so that they could hear all about the visit as soon as they returned. The conversation having ended with midday approaching they all set out towards the edge of the wood where the various relatives settled down to wait and Sammy, Browncoat, and Prickles headed for the warren which was situated beneath a slight mound on the side of the hill. At the entrance to the warren Thumper who had remained on watch whist the other rabbits went back underground greeted them and on instructing another rabbit to take his place and keep a careful eye out for intruders he led the way into the warren.

The warren had two entrances both of which were wide enough to allow two rabbits to pass and which narrowed after a short while and diverted into a number of much smaller tunnels. Thumper led them well into the warren where they were met by a large and much older rabbit with a distinguished look and grey whiskers. 'Welcome' said the rabbit 'my name is Greybeard and I am the chief of the warren. We have seen you from a distance from time to time and we really should have met before so let me show you round.' So off they set and the three friends were surprised at the amount of room that there was. There were a number of nurseries with a great deal of young rabbits and a similar amount of living areas for the adult rabbits. The warren was deep enough underground to avoid the worst of the frost during the winter and to keep cool in the summer. Sammy was impressed and said to Greybeard 'I had no idea that this warren was a large as it is, it is very well organised and there must be a lot of inhabitants but being so far out in the open on the hill does it not attract predators?' 'Yes it does' said Greybeard 'which is why we have Thumper here and his team who do a very good job of guarding us so to date we have not had a problem and the inhabitants of the wildwood have kept their distance.' 'That's fine' said Sammy 'but would it not be an idea to consider moving to the edge of our wood where you would be safer?' At this Greybeard pulled a face and said that rabbits had always had a warren here and that there did not appear to be a reason to move. Hearing this Samy diplomatically changed the subject back to general chatter. Just then there was a commotion and in rushed one of Thumper's rabbits.

Over at the wildwood the crows and ravens had been watching the warren from their nests in the pine trees. They saw the three friends go from their wood to the warren and also saw that there was only a single rabbit left at the entrance so one of them flew down and said to the foxes 'if you want to attack the warren now is the time to do it as there is only one rabbit there and it is being visited by three animals from the wood at the top of the hill.' 'That sounds good' said the chief fox 'so with luck we can kill several birds with one stone.' So he summoned all of the foxes, stoats, and weasels and told them the situation and they all agreed that now was the time to act so they all made their way to the edge of the wildwood and out onto the hill where unfortunately for them they were immediately spotted by Thumper's lookout who without further hesitation fled into the warren to report what was happening. What the foxes and their friends also didn't know was that various animals and particularly hedgehogs who were still gathered at the edge of the wood had also seen them.

Those gathered by the edge of the wood looked at each other in some consternation. 'What are we to do?' said a squirrel 'as the animals from the wildwood will make short work of both us and the voles?' 'Yes' said the hedgehogs 'but not of us so we will go to the warren and see what we can do' So off set some of the hedgehogs and although the foxes spotted them they took no notice as hedgehogs were not of any interest to them.

Back in the warren Thumper's lookout was telling both Thumper and Greybeard of the danger from the animals of the wildwood who were rapidly approaching. 'What are we to do' said Greybeard 'we have a lot of rabbits in the warren and they will all be in danger as we are no match for foxes especially when they have stoats and weasels with them.' 'Nonsense' said Sammy 'there is a lot we can do but we will have to be quick so these are my suggestions. First send your best diggers to block off one of the entrances so only the other can be attacked. Second as neither Browncoat or I can stand up to the wildwood animals I will ask Prickles to bring as many hedgehogs as he can find to help us and then to go over to the badger sett and see if they will come and chase off the foxes and their friends.' Browncoat and Prickles were listening and nodded their agreement and at that moment the sentry who had gone back to the entrance to the warren came rushing in saying that there were a number of hedgehogs outside wanting to warn us that the wildwood animals were coming and could they help.

Prickles then said 'I have an idea. If all the hedgehogs bunch together rolled up in a ball where the entrance narrows then no-one will be able to get in.' 'Excellent' said Sammy 'but we had better get a move on so Greybeard can you start your rabbits on blocking the other entrance please.'

By then the animals from the wildwood were close to the entrance to the warren but were just beaten to it by the hedgehogs which were too quick for them so they took no notice and all went into the warren where they could see both the rabbits and the friends and so lined up to attack. 'Wait' called out the chief fox 'there are two entrances so we had better look at both before we do anything else.' So some of them went to the second entrance and found the rabbits desperately trying to complete the blocking of the entrance who on seeing the intruders were going to flee leaving the blockage almost but not quite complete when Sammy called out to them to finish the blockage which then with some difficulty they did so the wildwood creatures were thwarted and returned to the main entrance where the hedgehogs had by now formed a barrier.

There were a lot of animals from the wildwood and Sammy could see that the hedgehogs couldn't hold them off for long so he said to Prickles 'I have another idea, why don't we ask the badgers for help as they are no friends of the wildwood creatures and they are only on the other side of the hill so Prickles as the foxes will not bother you could you go as quick as you can and ask for help?' Prickles thought for a moment and then said 'I think that is a splendid idea so I will set off now and see what I can do.' So off Prickles went and as Sammy had said the foxes avoided him as being too difficult to chase and not being of any account. Prickles then ran as fast as his very short legs would take him and in a short while he arrived at the badger's sett on the far side of the hill and on finding the entrance he shouted 'Is there anyone home?'

After a few moments a black and white striped face appeared followed by several other badgers all grumbling about being woken during the day. The first badger then said to Prickles 'Whatever brings you here when you know that badgers sleep during the day although I must say that the amount of noise coming from the wildwood has already disturbed us.' Prickles said to the badger 'we need your help as the wildwood creatures are attacking the rabbit warren on the other side of the hill and the rabbits are not strong enough to hold out for very long.' 'Is that so' said the badger 'for too long now the wildwood has been a nuisance along with all those who live there. They make too much noise and even try to come and share our sett but they are much too unruly for us so now is the time to deal with them once and for all before they try to take over all the hill which if they capture the rabbit warren I am sure they will.'

With that the badger called to all the other badgers and said to them 'I think we need to sort this out immediately so what do you think?' There was then a chorus of approval so a dozen or more large badgers set off towards the rabbit warren with Prickles trying hard to keep up!

In the meantime, things were not going so well at the warren. Although Sammy was trying to keep the wildwood creatures at bay it was a losing battle as the rabbits were of little help and the hedgehogs were tiring. 'Come on' said the chief fox 'one more effort and we'll be in the warren and then we shall have a tasty lunch' 'Hurrah cried the rest of the creatures and they launched another attack on the hedgehog wall which now began to crumble but just as they were about to break through there was a roar from the warren entrance and several of the weasels who were too small to help the larger creatures rushed in and said to the chief fox 'there are badgers outside and they are not at all friendly and are demanding that we stop this attack and go back to the wildwood.' 'Stuff and nonsense' said the chief fox 'we are in control and almost into the warren so I am not stopping for a few black and white striped creatures.' This however was a mistake as the badgers had followed the weasel into the warren and hearing what the chief fox said launched a fierce attack on the wildwood creatures. At this the weasels and the stoats immediately fled but the foxes being larger put up a fight but it was a losing battle against animals bigger and stronger than them so it was not long before only the chief fox was left facing the leader of the badgers. 'I suppose you think you are clever' he snarled 'but even if we retreat today we shall be back and will win and then we shall rule the hill and you will no longer matter.' 'That's just what we thought' said the leader of the badgers whilst the other badgers crowded round and nodded in agreement 'but you are underestimating us as we have been watching you and are tired of your behaviour and now that you have attacked the rabbit warren it is clear that there will be no safety for anyone until you are gone so we now give you a choice between leaving the wildwood or being trapped in the wildwood as we shall move our sett and surround the wood and make sure that you will not leave it again.'

'You wouldn't dare' said the chief fox 'there are too many of us for you to trap in the wildwood and we shall invade your sett and eventually chase you away' At that the leader of the badgers whose name was Brock said to the chief fox whose name was Vulpus 'then we will have the fight now and then we will see who is the stronger' and he moved menacingly closer to Vulpus and at the same time shouted to the other badgers 'round up the rest of the wildwood creatures' which they did. Vulpus then realised that the game was over and said to Brock 'so what now?' 'If I have my way both you and your wildwood will be destroyed' said Brock but at this point Sammy who had been on the edge of the fight now came forward and said 'no you can't do that although I agree that Vulpus and his friends will always be a nuisance so why don't we just banish them?'

'That's a good idea' said Brock so turning to Vulpus he said 'you heard what Sammy said so these are the terms. You have 24 hours to get all your families together and then leave the hill forever to wherever you can find but if you do not all of the badgers here along with others still in the sett will come after you as we are determined that there will be peace on the hill.' Seeing the situation Vulpus called to the remaining wildwood creatures and said to them 'I think our time is over so we had better sort ourselves out and leave' to which they agreed.

Just to finish this part of the story for those children that may be reading, Vulpus and the wildwood creatures left the hill within the 24-hour period and travelled for many days to find somewhere else to live. Eventually some way to the east of the hill they found an area of high moorland where no other creatures lived and there they settled and never returned to the hill.

The fight was finished and the rabbits came out of the warren to congratulate the badgers and Sammy for saving them. The badgers took this very gracefully saying that they had quite enjoyed coming out of their sett and were very pleased to see the back of the wildwood creatures as without them the hill would again be peaceful and quiet as the crows and ravens would no longer call to one another without them. They then left the warren to return to their sett as now it was late afternoon and they needed to rest before their usual nighttime excursions but said that they would visit more often to see how things were in the warren and the wood.

Once the badgers had gone Sammy said to Greybeard 'you have had a lucky escape and what has happened only shows how vulnerable the warren is being sited here so you ought to think seriously about moving closer to the wood. On one side of the wood there is a high bank that is ideal for a new warren and you would be surrounded by friends from the wood should the wildwood ever be a threat again and as a bonus we shall see more of you.' Greybeard thought for a moment and then said 'I think that given what has happened and what a close shave it was you are right' and the rest of the rabbits nodded in agreement.

So to finish this part of the story the rabbits set to work on digging a new warren and in a short space of time it was complete and they moved in after levelling their old warren and turning it back into pasture. The wildwood was not inhabited again and after a while it became greener and flowers began to grow so it became much more attractive. The crows and the ravens gradually moved out and were replaced by many smaller songbirds which particularly in the spring brightened up the wood.

Sammy, Browncoat, and Prickles returned to their wood where they were greeted by the other animals who were very relieved that the wildwood creatures were gone. 'Time for tea' said Sammy 'it's been a busy day and I'm hungry' so off he went to uncover a store of nuts while Browncoat and Prickles both nosed around for bugs and so a good time was had by all for the rest of the day.

The three friends again they went out
And did hear the rabbits all shout
We are being attacked
But do have a lack
Of resources to just stop the rout

3

The Moonbeam

The branches of the trees in the wood now stripped of their leaves stretched their bare bones to the night sky and rubbed them uneasily together as if to find what warmth there might be available. It was mid-winter and the nights were well below freezing and lit cloudlessly by the myriad of stars loitering in the galaxy like small Chinese lanterns. The summer colours were long gone buried beneath the floor of the wood snug against the cold waiting for the warmth of spring to entice them back above ground. The floor of the wood was covered with the tree's summer clothing now faded brown and curled against the frost so that when walked on they crackled and told everyone that something was about.

At this time of the year many animals were asleep living on the fat that they had stored up during the warm months of the year and hibernating safely against any passing predators of which in the wood there were very few now that the wildwood was empty. The hustle and bustle of the other seasons was replaced with quieter sounds. During the day the rabbits who now burrowed on the edge of the wood spread out onto the hill and browsed on the grass and at night the deer who slept in the wood during the day came out and browsed on the grass left by the rabbits and grazed on the hedgerows.

The smaller mammals such as mice, voles, and shrews were awake but kept within the wood in case during the day they might be spotted by a hungry hawk or during the night by a passing owl all of which found hunting that much easier when the trees were without leaves as their prey was more easily seen.

On one of those cold nights Sammy was restless and couldn't sleep so eventually waking he scuttled down the tree from his drey to see if he could find Browncoat in his hole at the foot of the tree. 'Are you awake?' called Sammy. After a while a somewhat sleepy voice replied 'What on earth are you doing up at this time of the night when you should be tucked up in bed?' Ah is that you Browncoat' said Sammy 'I couldn't sleep so I thought we might see what goes on in the wood at this time of night so shall we wake up Prickles so all three of us can explore?' 'Prickles might not be too pleased' said Browncoat 'as he sleeps more than us at this time of the year but we can but try although why you cannot sleep and want to go out in this temperature and at this time of night is quite beyond me.'

So off the two of them went to where Prickles lived under the holly bush and called out to him to see if he was awake and again after a while a very grumpy Prickles appeared wanting to know why on earth did the two of them need to wake him. 'Come on' said Sammy 'there will not be too many nights like this when it is clear and the stars provide some light and you never know but the moon might come out if we are lucky.' 'Lucky my foot' said Browncoat and Prickles 'and if it wasn't for my extra thick coat and Prickles extra layer of fat neither of us would even be talking to you but just this time we'll humour you but only if you promise to wait until the spring before you dream up any more madcap schemes like this.'

Nothing daunted Sammy said to them 'very well so let's go out onto the hill and see what's going on as nothing will be happening in the wood.' So off they set although Browncoat was worried as he was the smallest of the three of them and very open to being snapped up by a hungry owl so when they reached the open hill he said to the other two 'I can see deer further out on the hill so I will keep to the side of the wood while you go and have a chat.' 'Vey well' said Sammy 'although I think that you are being over cautious so we will catch up with you here later.' Then off went Sammy and Prickles and came up to the herd of deer who were grazing. 'Goodness me' said the chief buck 'what are you two doing here at this time of night?'

'I couldn't sleep' said Sammy 'so we thought we would come and see what is going on as we do not often come out at night.' 'Well' said the Buck 'all we do is graze and browse and tonight we are grazing whilst our fauns are playing as you can see.' At that moment the few clouds that were in the sky cleared and out shone the moon and bathed everything in light. The wood stood out in stark relief but without what little colour that it had at this time of the year rather like a black and white movie and although all the animals had seen the moon before on this occasion it was much brighter than normal.

'Goodness' said Sammy 'what a sight.' 'Yes' said the buck 'and there is Brock come to see what is going on.' 'What is happening?' said Brock coming up to the deer, Sammy, and Prickles. 'The moon does not normally shine as brightly as this and we can almost see as far as we can during the day.' 'What fun' chipped in Prickles who as a hedgehog was used to being around at night 'now we can both eat and play without any fear of being preyed on by owls as we can easily see them coming.'

In the meantime, Browncoat was keeping to the edge of the wood particularly as he could hear owls hooting. He too saw the moon come out but unlike Prickles thought to himself that that made it easier for the owls to see him and others like him and more difficult for him to hide and sure enough at that moment a dark shape descended from the sky with talons outstretched and plunged towards Browncoat who only just in time saw it and scampered into a nearby burrow.

The owl could not pull up in time and landed with a thump by the entrance to the burrow where it glared fiercely in frustration at Browncoat. 'Don't worry' said the owl 'I am not called Whispering Death for nothing and I'll get you next time and if I don't one of my friends will as we are all very hungry and there are many nice fat mice, voles, and shrews here in the wood to be caught.' At that knowing that Browncoat was now too alert to be caught for its supper the owl flew off to hunt for other prey leaving Browncoat very shaken and not knowing how to move from the burrow. 'Oh dear' he said to himself 'how silly I was to listen to the others and be persuaded to come out of the wood where I was safe. Now I may well have to stay here until the morning when the owls have gone to roost and I shall be safe again.'

But that at that moment the moon suddenly shone brighter still and there was a tremendous flash and at the same time a great beam of light reached down from the sky and struck the ground just a little distance from where Browncoat was sheltering in the burrow and just for a moment he was stunned and unable to move however recovering from the shock he collected his wits and looked carefully out of the burrow. To his surprise Browncoat saw what looked like a shining staircase stretching down from the sky to the hill just outside of the wood and to his greater surprise at the foot of the shining staircase he saw several small elf-like figures looking around as if to see where they were. On spotting Browncoat one of them beckoned his companions and they made their way over to him.

'Don't be frightened' said the first elf 'we shall not harm you as we are moon-elves and this is our moonbeam but we should not really be here and are not sure as to exactly where we are so can you please tell us.' Browncoat looked at the elves in some disbelief but listening to the tone of the elf's voice he was no longer afraid but said to the elf 'If I come out of this burrow the owl may return and then I shall be in trouble so it would be better if I stay where I am but I am happy to tell you where you are.' 'Don't worry' said the elf 'whilst we are here the owls will not attack and if they try it will be the worse for them so you can safely come out of the burrow before all this commotion wakes up the rabbits.'

So Browncoat came partly out of the burrow and thought that he would now be able to see his friends and the deer but little did he know that they too had seen the beam of light and were so frightened that they had fled back to the safety of the wood whilst the badgers had equally quickly made their way back to their sett underground. Once in the wood Sammy and Prickles recovered their senses and said to one another that they were safe enough but what about Browncoat? Sammy thought about looking on the outskirts of the wood but the light from the moonbeam was shining brightly and scared them from leaving the wood so he said to Prickles 'I am sure that Browncoat is safe in one of the burrows and that the rabbits will look after him if necessary so I think we should wait until the morning when things return to normal as after all he will be quite safe as no predators will dare hunt while it is as bright as this.' And bright it was as the light showed up the wood in stark relief – in other words children all the trees were shown up in their winter clothing and the shadows cast by their trunks were darker than normal – and the owls and other predators but mainly the owls were now hiding as far into the wood as they could go.

In the meantime, Browncoat had come right out of his burrow and recovering his wits said to the elf who had now been joined by several others 'this is the hill where I and my friends live. It is a long way from anything else and is normally very peaceful except at night when the owls are about. The hill has the wood which you can see behind me and the hill itself is home to both rabbits and badgers but what brings you here and where do you live?' 'thank you for that' said the elf 'as we are rather lost and shall probably be in trouble when we report back to the Chief of the Moon as we are normally well away from the ground up in the sky but we lost our way and landed here and it is just as well that your hill is so far away from anything else as we have no wish to have to explain ourselves to Men but in order to return we shall need your help.'

'My help' said Browncoat 'I don't know anything about you or your moonbeam so I don't see how I can help.' 'Oh but you can' replied the elf 'because although you know nothing of us you do know all about where we are which we do not and we need particular circumstances to return to the skies about which you can tell us.' 'Well' said Browncoat doubtfully 'ask away and I will do what I can.'

The elf then said 'our problem is that we are only here because we became lost and normally no-one is aware that we exist but having now landed here everyone may come to know that we exist as we are sure that the other animals who were frightened when we landed are now looking out from wherever they are hiding and will have seen us and will be able to tell others what they have seen. So you see we need you to keep quiet about this meeting and persuade your friends to do likewise.' Browncoat thought for a minute then he said 'I think that I had better call some of the other animals and see what they have to say. As far as I am concerned there is not a problem in that I shall not tell anyone about tonight and our meeting.'

So Browncoat called out to see if Sammy and Prickles were near and within a few moments they cautiously appeared along with several other animals and birds who had been awoken and also the badgers. Browncoat then explained what had been happening and introduced the chief elf who added to the explanation and repeated his request that what had happened not be circulated outside of the hill. The various animals and birds thought about it for a moment and then Brock said 'I think I speak for us all in saying that we will keep all of this to ourselves as if we do not there will be too much interest in us from those who we do not want.' All of the others nodded in agreement but then there was a hoot and down swept Whispering Death the owl which had frightened Browncoat and perching on a fencepost he looked fiercely at everyone and sneered at them 'you do not speak for me or the other owls as we are happy for others to invade the hill as it will make it easier for us to hunt and more difficult for you to defend it so we will broadcast it wherever we can and if that makes life difficult for you elves well that is just bad luck and you will have to live with it as our only concern is us.' 'Oh is that so' said the chief elf 'well I think you under-estimate what we elves can do. We have the ear of the Chief of the Moon and can ensure that he directs moonbeams wherever we tell him. You owls rely on hunting at night in the dark so as you are being so difficult I shall arrange for a moonbeam to be directed at you every night regardless of the weather which will prevent you from hunting so just let me show you.'

At that he drew out a wand from his belt and waved it once at the moonbeam which was still on the hill and then a band of light appeared which was directed by the elf to shine on the owls and particularly Whispering Death all of whom cowered away from it. 'Turn it off' said Whispering Death 'we don't like the light as we cannot hunt unless it is dark.' 'That' said the elf 'is the whole idea and unless you stop harassing the animals in the wood that band of light will always shine on you so you might as well go and live somewhere else.' Whispering Death looked at the other owls who nodded so he shrugged his wings and said to the elf 'very well you win so we will leave as there are other places where we can live which will suit us.' That is probably the best solution' said the elf but remember that if you mention to anyone as to what you have seen we shall be aware and will send the light to shine on you again.' With that shading their eyes with their wings the owls gathered together and flew away off of the hill and were not seen there again.

'That's a great relief' said Browncoat to the elf 'the hill will be a safer place thanks to you.' 'No thanks needed' said the elf as without your help we should have had a problem so as a reward would you like to climb the moonbeam and see how we live which we will be happy to show you as a reward for your help. 'Yes please' said Browncoat and can Sammy and prickles come as well please as we do most things together?' 'Well I don't suppose two more will matter' said the elf 'so yes they can if they wish.' So Browncoat turned to his two friends and asked them if they would like to come with him up the moonbeam and without hesitation both of them said yes. So the elf again waved his wand and the beam of light merged with the main moonbeam to form a staircase skywards.

'Follow me' said the elf and he and the other elves went to the foot of the moonbeam and prepared to climb up. When Browncoat and his friends joined them the chief elf tapped the three of them gently on the head and said to them 'that will make sure that you can climb and not fall through so off we go.'

So off they all set, the three friends very cautiously at first as they thought that they were bound to fall through and if they did then as they were not far off the ground that they would not come to much harm however to their surprise they found that it was firm beneath their feet and the climbing was very easy. After a short while still following the elves they saw that the moonbeam ended in a small cloud which they had not noticed before. 'Come on' said the chief elf 'this is where we live which is always hidden by this cloud so that nobody would know what is behind it. I will show you around and then before the dawn comes and you return to the hill you will meet the chief of the moon.' So very nervously the three friends headed by Browncoat stepped off the moonbeam and onto the cloud. As they came onto the cloud the light became much brighter and they could no longer see the hill below and on gazing in awe they saw not far away a castle gleaming in the light.

'How is it that we could not see this from the hill?' all three of them asked. 'Well that is because we keep ourselves hidden from prying eyes' said the chief elf 'so now come with me and you shall meet the Chief of the Moon in his castle but hurry as the dawn is not that far away.' So off they set through a mystical world of white, shining, fluffy cloud-cover the wisps of which curled around their feet and in a short time they came to the entrance of the castle which was guarded by two other elves. 'Who goes there' called the guards 'friends' said the chief elf so in they all went and were then escorted by a very grand elf to the throne room where on a raised platform the King of the Moon sat on a grand throne.

The King was dressed in white flowing robes and had a long white well manicured beard and a jewelled crown on his head. 'Welcome to our world' said the King 'I hear that the three of you and particularly Browncoat have saved us from a difficult situation so I am grateful and as a reward I will make sure that you are no longer bothered by predators such as owls during the night and will send an envoy to my friend the Emperor of the Sun to ask if he can do the same for you during the day. Now much that I would like to talk further with you the dawn fast approached and we need to be away and you need to return to your hill so once again our thanks for your help and goodbye.' The three friends were almost too overcome to reply but Sammy plucked up courage and thanked the King for what he had done for them and said again that neither they nor anyone else on the hill would breathe a word of the night's happenings.

At this the grand elf came forward and guided the three friends through the castle corridors back to the chief of the elves and said his goodbyes. 'You have been very fortunate' said the chief of the elves 'there are very few who have been granted an audience with the King of the Moon and fewer still those who have spoken to him.' The elf then led the way back to the moonbeam which was still in place and said to them 'The dawn is about to break so we cannot escort you back to the hill but the moonbeam will remain solid for as long as it is dark so you just need to follow it down and all will be well so goodbye, it has been good to meet you and perhaps one night we shall meet again.'

So off set the three friends and not before time as just as they were back on the hill the first slivers of dawn were showing and the moonbeam immediately vanished. 'My goodness that was a close shave' said Browncoat 'but now we are safely back and with luck will not be bothered by owls and their like again.' By now the light was coming up and the frost was heavy on the grass but the sun was rising in the east and promised a bright winter's day perhaps as a reward for all their efforts during the night. 'My goodness I'm tired' said Browncoat and Sammy and Prickles agreed. 'I shouldn't really be up at all said Prickles so I am off back to bed.' So off he went back to the holly bush where he lived, rolled himself into a ball, and off he went to sleep.

Sammy said to Browncoat' I think I shall have some breakfast and then spend the day dozing in the warmth of my drey as it was a busy night.' And Browncoat agreed so off they both went and both looked forward to adventures to come.

The three friends were up in the night
Because all of the hill were in fright
As no-one had seen
An elf or a beam
Of light that rose up in the night

Available worldwide from Amazon

Michael Terence
Publishing

www.mtp.agency

mtp.agency

@mtp_agency

Printed in Great Britain
by Amazon

50023024R00046